How to Interpret Any Dream

APOSTLE JOSEPH PRUDE

How To Interpret Any Dream

Copyright © 2015 by Joseph L. Prude

Cover Designed by JOSEP Book Designs *(joseworkwork@gmail.com)*

Edited by: Apostle Barbara W. Erkins
Formatted by: Apostle Sandra Prude Formatted by: Apostle Noreen Battle

Scripture quotations are from:
The Holy Bible, King James Version, Holman Christian Standard Bible, and the American Standard Version
Visit the author's website at: www.AJP Ministries.com

Printed in the United States of America

Contents

CHAPTER ONE

HOW TO INTERPRET
ANY DREAM

Daniel 1:17 (KJV)

> *17 As for these four children, God gave them knowledge and skill in all learning and wisdom: and Daniel had understanding in all visions and dreams.*

Looking at this verse from the book of Daniel, we readily see that the scripture highlights the skill level of Daniel and his friends as it pertained to dream interpretation... they were "that good."

While dream interpretation may involve some gifting, it is not just a gift as many think. What does encompass dream interpretation, though, is work, diligence and effort. Unfortunately, one cannot acquire this skill through the laying on of hands. This skill comes strictly through the repetitive activity of honing the craft of interpretation. So, if you desire to become a skilled dream interpreter, then you must know it will require you to put in much effort and labor in the journey. When we allow dreams to go uninterpreted, we have allowed the 'uploading' of many life changing and invaluable gifts to simply be thrown away. Therefore, it is of critical importance for a believer to develop the tools to interpret his or her own dreams.

In this short book we will teach you some very simple lessons and give you access to powerful tools that will put you well on your way to being able to interpret your dreams. If you will use these tools repetitively, as you interpret dreams, you will see a noticeable increase in your skill and confidence level. I personally use these tools in my own time of dream interpretation and have found them very effective as they unlock the mystery of just about any and every dream I have.

PROPHETIC WORD

The word of Lord comes and says, "My people, it is my desire that you know the mysteries of the kingdom. This is not the age of hidden things; this is the age of revealed things, I reveal the dark and hidden things to those who have a desire to know." The Lord says, "Many have lost great treasures, answers to prayer and divine instructions, because they did not know how to interpret their dreams."

Chapter Two

The Dream Interpreter's Tool Kit

There are several different tools that you will need in order to be effective in dream interpretation

1. **The word of wisdom**

   1 Corinthians 12:7-8 (KJV)

   [7] The manifestation of the Spirit is given to every man to profit withal.

   [8] For to one is given by the Spirit the word of wisdom; to another the word of knowledge by the same Spirit;

The word of wisdom takes the similitudes of the spirit and makes them understandable. Without the ability to access the word of wisdom for dream interpretation, dreams would hold no value. The word of wisdom is like a decoding device. It takes mysteries out of heaven, out of the spirit realm, and brings them to earth so they may be understood.

If you will notice in verse 13 of 1 Corinthians 2, you see the phrase that says, *"...which things also we speak, not in the words which man's wisdom teacheth, but which the Holy Ghost teacheth, comparing spiritual things with spiritual."*

In other words, one of the ways to interpret dreams means to speak a dream out audibly and then allow the dream to be spoken out of your mouth in a prophetic fashion. Thus, the word of wisdom will work to bring the interpretation of the dream. In fact, in Thayer's dictionary the word of wisdom actually means to interpret a dream or dream interpretation.

1 Corinthians 2:8-13 (KJV)

[8] Which none of the princes of this world knew: for had they known it, they would not have crucified the Lord of glory.

[9] But as it is written, Eye hath not seen, nor ear heard, neither have entered into the

heart of man, the things which God hath prepared for them that love him.

[10] But God hath revealed them unto us by his Spirit: for the Spirit searcheth all things, yea, the deep things of God.

[11] For what man knoweth the things of a man, save the spirit of man which is in him? Even so the things of God knoweth no man, but the Spirit of God.

[12] Now we have received, not the spirit of the world, but the spirit which is of God; that we might know the things that are freely given to us of God.

[13] Which things also we speak, not in the words which man's wisdom teacheth, but which the Holy Ghost teacheth; comparing spiritual things with spiritual.

2. **The Understanding of Similitudes.**

Hosea 12:10 (KJV)

[10] I have also spoken by the prophets and I have multiplied visions, and used similitude, by the ministry of the prophets.

Numbers 12:8 (KJV)

[8] With him will I speak mouth to mouth, even apparently, and not in dark speeches; and the similitude of the LORD shall he behold: wherefore then were ye not afraid to speak against my servant Moses?

The word similitude means to resemble or "to be like." Many things we see in dreams are similitudes and not literal. You will find it very rare that what you see in a dream is literal. For this reason it so important to understand similitudes. The first step toward understanding in this area is to get a good prophetic dictionary. There are several on the market, but allow me to suggest what I think is best and that is, "The Prophets Dictionary" by Dr. Paula Price. Secondly, you want to develop your own personal dictionary of symbols and similitudes.

The reason you want to have your own personal dictionary of symbols and similitudes is because there are two different classes of symbols and similitudes: there are objective symbols and subjective symbols. The objective symbol is one that is commonly known and can be interpreted from the scriptures. The subjective symbol is a symbol that only has meaning to you and would have no meaning for any other person. For example, if you were to see an old high school teacher in a dream, that teacher would have a specific meaning to you. To see the teacher in your dream would be a subjective symbol, one that only has specific meaning to you, but conversely, the function or the office of a teacher, in general, would have an objective meaning to everyone. Hence, it is so important to develop a personal dictionary of symbols or similitudes that has specific meaning for you.

3. A Dream Journal

Jeremiah 30:2 (KJV)

² Thus speaketh the LORD God of Israel, saying, Write thee all the words that I have spoken unto thee in a book.

To be effective in dream interpretation it is critical to have a dream journal. This journal is one in which you consistently and diligently record your dreams. The journal does not need to be fancy, just functional. The following subject matter is important to list in your dream journal:

1. Date of the dream

2. Subject of the dream

3. Was the dream in color or black and white?

4. Was there any scripture in the dream?

5. The dream itself

6. The present interpretation of the dream

7. Leave a place for the future interpretation of the dre

Chapter Three

Two Major Methods of Dream Interpretation

1. The Linear Method of Dream Interpretation

Mark 4:13 (KJV)

[13] And he said unto them, Know ye not this parable? And how then will ye know all parables?

The bible is a book of keys. In careful study of the scripture you will find that every seal can be opened and every locked door has a key. Jesus gives us one of these keys in the parable of the sower as found in Mark 4, in Matthew 13 and in Luke 8. When the disciples asked him about the meaning of this parable, he used this as an opportunity to tell them that it was not God's purpose that they should not see.

Mark 4:11 (KJV)

¹¹ And he said unto them, Unto you it is given to know the mystery of the kingdom of God: but they that are without, all things are done in parables.

He told them it is given to them to know the mystery of the kingdom. It is not for scripture to remain hidden, but to be both interpreted and understood. He then began to teach the linear method of interpretation.

The linear method is a process that involves several different steps. If this method is used properly then every dream, vision and parable can be interpreted. In the parable of the sower, we begin to see Jesus teach His disciples the linear method of interpretation. You will notice that Jesus begins to interpret this parable in a step by step method in which He identifies each symbol before He gives the interpretation.

Step 1.

He identifies the prophetic identity of the sower:

Mark 4:14 (KJV)

¹⁴ The sower soweth the word.

Step 2.

He identifies the prophetic identity of those by the way side:

> **Mark 4:15 (KJV)**
>
> *[15] And these are they by the way side, where the word is sown; but when they have heard, Satan cometh immediately, and taketh away the word that was sown in their hearts*

Step 3.

He identifies the prophetic meaning of the stony ground:

> **Mark 4:16 (KJV)**
>
> [16] And these are they likewise which are sown on stony ground; who, when they have heard the word, immediately receive it with gladness;

Step 4.

He identifies the prophetic meaning of the thorns:

> **Mark 4:18 (KJV)**

> *18 And these are they which are sown among thorns; such as hear the word,*

Step 5.

He identifies the prophetic meaning of the good ground:

Mark 4:20 (KJV)

> *20 And these are they which are sown on good ground; such as hear the word, and receive it, and bring forth fruit, some thirtyfold, some sixty, and some an hundred.*

You will notice that Jesus does not give a generalized interpretation of this parable. He uses the principle of line upon line and precept upon precept. Jesus interpreted this parable by lines and precepts. In other words, Jesus identified the meaning of each object in the parable, then the object's meaning or the precept that should come from the parable. This principle can be applied to any dream, any vision, etc., if you are able to identify each line of the dream and then interpret the precept. Jesus says this is the way we understand all parables (dreams). There are many that love to imply that every mystery, (in scripture), should remain a mystery, but the Comforter, the Holy Ghost, will teach us all things and lead us into all truth.

Chapter Four

DANIEL DEMONSTRATES THE LINEAR METHOD OF INTERPRETATION

It is amazing how accurate and consistent the scriptures are. Several hundred years before Jesus appears on the scene, we see Daniel's interpretation of dreams is by use of the same Linear Method.

Nebuchadnezzar's Dream

Daniel 4:9-27 (KJV)

⁹ O Belteshazzar, master of the magicians, because I know that the spirit of the holy gods is in thee, and no secret troubleth thee, tell me the visions of my dream that I have seen, and the interpretation thereof.

¹⁰ *Thus were the visions of mine head in my bed; I saw, and behold a tree in the midst of the earth, and the height thereof was great.*

¹¹ *The tree grew, and was strong, and the height thereof reached unto heaven, and the sight thereof to the end of all the earth:*

¹² *The leaves thereof were fair and the fruit thereof much, and in it was meat for all: the beasts of the field had shadow under it, and the fowls of the heaven dwelt in the boughs thereof, and all flesh was fed of it.*

¹³ *I saw in the visions of my head upon my bed, and, behold, a watcher and a holy one came down from heaven;*

¹⁴ *He cried aloud, and said thus, Hew down the tree, and cut off his branches, shake off his leaves, and scatter his fruit: let the beasts get away from under it, and the fowls from his branches:*

¹⁵ *Nevertheless leave the stump of his roots in the earth, even with a band of iron and brass, in the tender grass of the field; and*

let it be wet with the dew of heaven, and let his portion be with the beasts in the grass of the earth:

[16] *Let his heart be changed from man's, and let a beast's heart be given unto him; and let seven times pass over him.*

[17] *This matter is by the decree of the watchers, and the demand by the word of the holy ones: to the intent that the living may know that the most High ruleth in the kingdom of men, and giveth it to whomsoever he will, and setteth up over it the basest of men.*

[18] *This dream I king Nebuchadnezzar have seen. Now thou, O Belteshazzar, declare the interpretation thereof, forasmuch as all the wise men of my kingdom are not able to make known unto me the interpretation: but thou art able; for the spirit of the holy gods is in thee.*

[19] *Then Daniel, whose name was Belteshazzar, was astounded for one hour, and his thoughts*

troubled him. The king spake, and said, Belteshazzar, let not the dream, or the interpretation

thereof, trouble thee. Belteshazzar answered and said, My lord, the dream be to them that hate thee, and the interpretation thereof to thine enemies.

20 The tree that thou sawest, which grew, and was strong, whose height reached unto the heaven, and the sight thereof to all the earth;

21 Whose leaves were fair, and the fruit thereof much, and in it was meat for all; under which the beasts of the field dwelt, and upon whose branches the fowls of the heaven had their habitation:

22 It is thou, O king that art grown and become strong: for thy greatness is grown, and reacheth unto heaven, and thy dominion to the end of the earth.

23 And whereas the king saw a watcher and an holy one coming down from heaven, and

*saying, Hew the tree down, and destroy it;
yet leave the stump of the roots thereof in the
earth, even with a band of iron and brass, in
the tender grass of the field; and let it be wet
with the dew of heaven, and let his portion
be with the beasts of the field, till seven times
pass over him;*

[24] *This is the interpretation, O king, and
this is the decree of the most High, which is
come upon my lord the king:*

[25] *That they shall drive thee from men, and
thy dwelling shall be with the beasts of the
field, and they shall make thee to eat grass
as oxen, and they shall wet thee with the
dew of heaven, and seven times shall pass
over thee, till thou know that the most High
ruleth in the kingdom of men, and giveth it
to whomsoever he will.*

[26] *And whereas they commanded to leave the
stump of the tree roots; thy kingdom shall
be sure unto thee, after that thou shalt have
known that the heavens do rule.*

> *²⁷ Wherefore, O king, let my counsel be acceptable unto thee, and break off thy sins by righteousness, and thine iniquities by shewing mercy to the poor; if it may be a lengthening of thy tranquility.*

The keys that Daniel identified:

1. The king was the tree - verse 22

2. The meaning of the cutting down of the tree - verse 23

3. The meaning of the stump - verse 26

4. The meaning of the leaves and the fruit - verse 21

5. The hewing down of the tree - verse 23

6. The meaning of the band of iron - verse 26

7. The meaning of seven times - verse 25

Notice Daniel's statement in verse 24:

"This is the interpretation". Daniel simply indicated that all he had said prior to this was merely the unraveling and pointing out of keys. Once Daniel completed the unraveling, it was then time for the interpretation. Daniel's methodology aligns perfectly with the instruction we receive from scripture.

Isaiah 28:9-10 (KJV)

[9] Whom shall he teach knowledge? And whom shall he make to understand doctrine? Them that are weaned from the milk, and drawn from the breasts.

[10] For precept must be upon precept, precept upon precept; line upon line, line upon line; here a little, and there a little.

In order to fully understand doctrine, one must be aware that "understanding a thing" versus "reading a thing" are two very different principles. Dreams give understanding. Many times a dream acts as a basis for one to be made aware of what one already knows. This enlightened understanding, more often than not, can be taught with regard to dreams by the concept known as the linear method of dream interpretation; line upon line and precept upon precept.

Kimchi says

צו tsau, precept, is used here for הוצמ mitsuah, command, and is used in no other place for it but here. צו tsau signifies a little precept, such as is suited to the capacity of a child; see verse 9. קו kau signifies the line that a mason stretches out to build a layer of stones by. After one layer or course is placed, he raises the line and builds another; thus the building is by degrees regularly completed. This is the method of teaching children, giving them such information as their narrow capacities can receive

— Adam Clarke's Commentary

This method of interpretation, as stated by the commentator, is likened to the erecting of an architectural structure; it is done layer after layer. God has always dealt with man by an incremental layer by layer unveiling, as well. To understand this layer by layer unveiling is the key reason one needs to have access to the right dream interpretation material.

CHAPTER FIVE

JOSEPH DEMONSTRATES THE LINEAR INTERPRETATION METHOD

We all see this method of interpretation in the ministry of the Dream Master, Joseph. We see this when he interpreted the Baker's and the Cup Bearer's dreams.

Genesis 40:5-13 (KJV)

> ⁵ *And they dreamed a dream both of them, each man his dream in one night, each man according to the interpretation of his dream, the butler and the baker of the king of Egypt, which were bound in the prison.*

⁶ *And Joseph came in unto them in the morning, and looked upon them, and, behold, they were sad.*

⁷ *And he asked Pharaoh's officers that were with him in the ward of his lord's house, saying, Wherefore look ye so sadly to day?*

⁸ *And they said unto him, We have dreamed a dream, and there is no interpreter of it. And Joseph said unto them, Do not interpretations belong to God? Tell me them, I pray you.*

⁹ *And the chief butler told his dream to Joseph, and said to him, In my dream, behold, a vine was before me;*

¹⁰ *And in the vine were three branches: and it was as though it budded, and her blossoms shot forth; and the clusters thereof brought forth ripe grapes:*

¹¹ *And Pharaoh's cup was in my hand: and I took the grapes, and pressed them into Pharaoh's cup, and I gave the cup into Pharaoh's hand.*

¹² And Joseph said unto him, This is the interpretation of it: The three branches are three days:

¹³ Yet within three days shall Pharaoh lift up thine head, and restore thee unto thy place: and thou shalt deliver Pharaoh's cup into his hand, after the former manner when thou wast his butler.

1. Three branches three days

He used the linear method to identify the meaning of the branches and then by the word of wisdom, Joseph was able to interpret the rest of the dream. If you look carefully on the surface, there was no mention made of the butler's restored position or anything beyond the blossoms, the vine, and the branches.

Genesis 40:16-19 (KJV)

¹⁶ When the chief baker saw that the interpretation was good, he said unto Joseph, I also was in my dream, and, behold, I had three white baskets on my head:

¹⁷ And in the uppermost basket there was of all manner of bake meats for Pharaoh;

and the birds did eat them out of the basket upon my head.

[18] And Joseph answered and said, This is the interpretation thereof: The three baskets are three days:

[19] Yet within three days shall Pharaoh lift up thy head from off thee, and shall hang thee on a tree; and the birds shall eat thy flesh from off thee.

2. Three baskets three days

Joseph first identifies the baskets as three days, then he uses the word of wisdom to bring the rest of interpretation of the dream. The linear method of interpretation in conjunction with the word of wisdom is a very powerful means of interpretation. We see this again in the ministry of Joseph when he interprets Pharaohs dream. He uses the linear method of interpretation in conjunction with the word of wisdom

Chapter Six

The Linear Interpretation of Pharaoh's Dream

Genesis 41:25-27 (ASV)

[25] And Joseph said unto Pharaoh, The dream of Pharaoh is one: what God is about to do he hath declared unto Pharaoh.

[26] The seven good kine are seven years; and the seven good ears are seven years: the dream is one.

[27] And the seven lean and ill-favored kine that came up after them are seven years, and also the seven empty ears blasted with

the east wind; they shall be seven years of famine.

1. The seven good kine = seven years

2. The seven good ears = seven years

3. The seven lean and ill – favored kine = seven years

4. Seven empty ears blasted with the east wind = seven years of famine

As you read carefully in verse 28 you readily see Joseph begins to shift gears. He begins to speak first person in a prophetic word of wisdom. Listen carefully.

Genesis 41:28 (ASV)

28 That is the thing which I spake unto Pharaoh: what God is about to do he hath showed unto Pharaoh.

"This is the thing that I have spake unto Pharaoh." The grammatical usage we see here means this was a first person prophetic word of wisdom. God spoke through the mouth of Joseph and said "this is what I have spoken". If you will, notice two words in this verse, the word ***thing*** and the word ***spoke***. The Hebrew word for speak is the word ***dabar***. It is very interesting to note the root word for (dabar) means to be behind or back chamber. In other words, to speak from behind or speak the past. This confirms the fact that this was a prophetic word of wisdom speaking to Pharaoh of what was already said. Joseph begins to speak in the word of wisdom giving Pharaoh divine instructions. Listen to this counsel that flows out of the mouth of Joseph.

Genesis 41:29-39 (KJV)

29 Behold, there come seven years of great plenty throughout all the land of Egypt:

30 And there shall arise after them seven years of famine; and all the plenty shall be forgotten in the land of Egypt; and the famine shall consume the land;

31 And the plenty shall not be known in the land by reason of that famine following; for it shall be very grievous.

32 And for that the dream was doubled unto Pharaoh twice; it is because the thing is established by God, and God will shortly bring it to pass.

[33] Now therefore let Pharaoh look out a man discreet and wise, and set him over the land of Egypt.

[34] Let Pharaoh do this, and let him appoint officers over the land, and take up the fifth part of the land of Egypt in the seven plenteous years.

[35] And let them gather all the food of those good years that come, and lay up corn under the hand of Pharaoh, and let them keep food in the cities.

[36] And that food shall be for store to the land against the seven years of famine, which shall be in the land of Egypt; that the land perish not through the famine.

[37] And the thing was good in the eyes of Pharaoh, and in the eyes of all his servants.

[38] And Pharaoh said unto his servants, Can we find such a one as this is, a man in whom the Spirit of God is?

*[39] And Pharaoh said unto Joseph, Forasmuch
as God hath shewed thee all this, there is
none so discreet and wise as thou art:*

Once a dream is broken into pieces by use of the linear
method, it is then critical that the word of wisdom operates
in such a manner as to bring the sense and meaning of
all that was identified in the linear method. If you will
notice, it was only after Joseph broke down each part and
spoke by the word of wisdom that the meaning of the
dream and the impact of that dream saved the future of
an entire nation.

CHAPTER SEVEN

THE WORD OF
WISDOM METHOD

1 Corinthians 2:6a (KJV)

> *⁶ Howbeit we speak wisdom among them*
> *that are perfect:*

We have shown you how the linear method works. Now we will get down to "brass tacks" in how the word of wisdom is best used in dream interpretation. When the word of wisdom is used, the meaning of the dream should be spoken out in a prophetic flow. It is important to remember that this is not the anointing of wisdom, as spoken of in the book of Isaiah, but the word of wisdom. It is a supernatural release of insight and knowledge by utterance.

1 Corinthians 12:8 (KJV)

[8] For to one is given by the Spirit the word of wisdom; to another the word of knowledge by the same Spirit;

The word of wisdom is another very powerful tool in dream interpretation. To understand how this operates in dream interpretation, we must first understand what the word of wisdom is. The word of wisdom is often misunderstood. The word of wisdom operates in many aspects of ministry though, in a hidden way.

Ways the word wisdom operates are as follows:

1. In preaching

2. In prophetic utterance

3. In song

4. In the ministry of the Psalmist

5. In counseling

6. In administration

7. In prophetic arts

8. In poetry

9. Dream interpretation

10. Dissolving doubts and explaining riddles

The operation of the word of wisdom in dream interpretation is indeed very powerful. This is different than the linear method of interpretation. The linear method is more rational and contemplative. The method of interpreting by the word of wisdom is more inspirational. We see this method employed in the ministry of Joseph, the Dream Master. It's different from what we saw in Daniel.

1 Corinthians 2:6-7 (KJV)

[6] Howbeit we speak wisdom among them that are perfect: yet not the wisdom of this world, nor of the princes of this world, that come to nought:

[7] But we speak the wisdom of God in a mystery, even the hidden wisdom, which God ordained before the world unto our glory

The word of wisdom is similar to prophesying. It is the same flow or operation of the spirit, however, one is speaking wisdom to interpret a dream.

Getting to the "WHAT" and the "WHY" of a dream is most assuredly a treasure hunt with one exception: interpretation can sometimes be a gift of the Spirit. "For to one is given by the Spirit the word of wisdom," (I Cor. 12:8).

From Thayer's Dictionary, the gift of the Spirit, that is "word of wisdom," encompasses more than prudence, full intelligence, and skillful management. The Greek word for wisdom, *sophia*, includes in its meaning: "the act of interpreting dreams and always giving the sagest advice and the intelligence evidenced in discovering the meaning of some mysterious number or vision."

The various ways the Word of Wisdom operates in dream interpretation are as follows:

1. Spoken out like a prophetic word

2. A general quick insight as to what the dream means

3. Unlocking the meaning of subjective similitudes

4. Making the dream applicable to the dreamer

5. Harmonizing various parts of a dream

Example in the ministry of Joseph:

Genesis 41:32-36 (KJV)

[32] And for that the dream was doubled unto Pharaoh twice; it is because the thing is established by God, and God will shortly bring it to pass.

[33] Now therefore let Pharaoh look out a man discreet and wise, and set him over the land of Egypt.

[34] Let Pharaoh do this, and let him appoint officers over the land, and take up the fifth part of the land of Egypt in the seven plenteous years.

[35] And let them gather all the food of those good years that come, and lay up corn under the hand of Pharaoh, and let them keep food in the cities.

> *36 And that food shall be for store to the land against the seven years of famine, which shall be in the land of Egypt; that the land perish not through the famine.*

Joseph tells Pharaoh the practical application of the dream and he did this by speaking it out through the word of wisdom

Example of word of wisdom delivered by a prophetic word:

Genesis 41:25-28 (KJV)

> *25 And Joseph said unto Pharaoh, The dream of Pharaoh is one: God hath shewed Pharaoh what he is about to do.*

> *26 The seven good kine are seven years; and the seven good ears are seven years: the dream is one.*

> *27 And the seven thin and ill favoured kine that came up after them are seven years; and the seven empty ears blasted with the east wind shall be seven years of famine.*

> *28 This is the thing which I have spoken unto Pharaoh: What God is about to do he sheweth unto Pharaoh.*

We see Joseph's change of phraseology in verse 28 and how it impacts the entire flow: "This is the thing that I have spoken unto Pharaoh." This is no longer Joseph speaking in and of himself, but this a prophetic word that came out of the mouth of Joseph as God spoke through him in what is called a first person prophetic utterance. In other words, you will speak out the meaning of the dream. This is the word of wisdom method of dream interpretation.

CHAPTER EIGHT

MAKING IT SIMPLE

Step One

Write the dream down or record the dream on a tape recorder as soon as you awaken so that you don't lose the dream. If the dream is recorded on a tape recorder, then take time to physically write out the dream. Please understand that to write out the dream is a very important step in dream interpretation. Do not write the dream down on just any piece of paper you happen to find. To do so indicates that you are not serious about dream interpretation. If you are serious about dream interpretation, then get a journal, so you will have a specific place where you will record your dreams according to the formula aforementioned.

Step Two

Now that the dream is written, the next step is to go through the linear method of interpretation. As we have already clearly stated, you want to go to each symbol in the dream and decode or interpret what each individual symbol means. It is in this part of the process of dream interpretation we must remember to be keenly aware of the difference between objective symbols and subjective symbols. Make sure you do this as studiously and as wisely as possible. Do not rush through this portion of your dream interpretation time. As you do this interpretation, you need to be accurate. It may prove necessary for you to take out any prophetic dictionaries that you have on hand, as well as your own subjective prophetic dictionary which includes the symbols which have only meaning to you.

Step Three

At this point, each and every symbol in the dream has been decoded by use of the linear method. Next, you want to take all of the individual symbols, and bring them together in order to realize a general line of thought that connects the symbols. As Jesus has already promised, if you use this method you will never have a dream that you cannot interpret.

Step Four

The next step is to use the word of wisdom method to speak out the meaning of the dream. It is of the utmost importance that one be able to use this method in one's dream interpretation. I will, therefore, add that one needs to understand how to flow in a prophetic dimension. If you come from a school of thought or theological background that teaches you cannot flow freely in a prophetic dimension, you may find this particular aspect of dream interpretation difficult for you. I will, however, make the case for my argument in saying I believe we have plainly proven scripturally that this is a most needed method in order to be effective in dream interpretation.

Step Five

Once you have used these two methods, (the linear method and the word of wisdom method), to interpret your dream, make sure that you keep a record of the dream and that you pray over the dream, and periodically review the dream. As time passes and you are committed to the use of these methods, you will find that you will continue to grow and mature in your ability to interpret dreams. As you move into the future with greater skill and acumen in dream interpretation, you will make a discovery. As you go back and review some of your former dreams, you may sense the Holy Spirit will prompt you to re-interpret a dream you formerly interpreted; however, you may discover there are new levels of insight into that same dream.

Step Six

One of the things that you want to also do is what we call "dream mapping." Take a look at your dreams that have occurred over a period of time and review them in order to see if there is a consistent line of thought or message contained within a particular set of dreams in a certain time frame. This is dream mapping, where you find there is a reoccurring message flowing through a particular set of dreams within a certain time frame.

Chapter Nine

Conclusion

I hope this book helps you reap the valuable harvest that is in the dreams that the Lord has given to you. Remember, learning to interpret dreams is a developed spiritual skill. You will be more skilled as you are diligent in "dream interpretation." As you become more skilled, the Holy Spirit will increase the complexity of your dreams so that your skill will likewise increase. The tools that we have laid out in this handbook will help you enjoy the rich river of revelation that is to be found in this dimension of communication with the Lord.

PROPHETIC WORD

I hear the Lord say

"My precious ones, it is My great desire to speak to you on many levels. The realm of dreams is one of the places that I can fellowship with you and give you insight and access to My voice. My precious child, take these truths and run with all that you have into this chamber of light. I will meet you here and you will never be the same,"

Saith the Lord of the Dream

NOTES

_____

_____

_____

_____

_____

_____

_____

_____

_____

_____

_____

Apostle Joseph Prude

_____

_____

_____

_____

_____

_____

_____

_____

_____

_____

_____

_____

_____

_____

_____

_____

_____

_____

_____

_____

_____

_____

_____

_____

_____

_____

_____

_____

_____

_____

_____

_____

_____

_____

_____

_____

_____

_____

_____

_____

_____

Book Orderring Information

Other Books Written By: Chief Apostle Joseph L. Prude

Prophetic Laboratory

Office of the Dream Master

Dream Masters College Curriculum

Female Apostle

The False Bishop

Restoring Healing in The African American Church

The Creation

Ministry of the Apostle

Office of the Chief Apostle

Ministry of the Prophet

Ministry of the Prophet Level 2

The Certified Prophetic Trainer

The Highjacking of the Gospel

The Secrets of His Presence

The Mystery of Angels

The False Teaching of the Tallit

How to Interpret Any Dream

Interracial Marriage

Prophetic Proverbs

The Ministry of Fasting and Prayer

josephprude@gmail.com

Order books on amazon.com

or

www.ajpministries.com

Made in the USA
Middletown, DE
22 September 2022

11048040R00035